T0039980

BLUESTONE

FARRAR, STRAUS AND GIROUX

NEW YORK

BLUESTONE

NEW AND SELECTED POEMS

JAMES LASDUN

Farrar, Straus and Giroux
18 West 18th Street, New York 10011

Published simultaneously in hardcover and paperback
First edition, 2015

Grateful acknowledgment is made for permission to reprint the following: Poems from *A Jump Start* by James Lasdun. Copyright © 1987 by James Lasdun. Used by permission of W. W. Norton & Company, Inc. Poems from *Woman Police Officer in Elevator* by James Lasdun. Copyright © 1997 by James Lasdun. Used by permission of W. W. Norton & Company, Inc. Poems from *Landscape with Chainsaw* by James Lasdun. Copyright © 2001 by James Lasdun. Used by permission of W. W. Norton & Company, Inc.

Many of these poems have appeared (some in slightly different form) in the following publications: *The Atlantic, Boulevard, Columbia Magazine, Encounter, Fiction, Granta, The Literary Review, Little Star, London Review of Books, The New Yorker, New Writing, The Observer* (London), *The Paris Review, Pequod, Poetry, The Poetry Review, Soho Square, Subtropics, The Times Literary Supplement, TriQuarterly, TWOFOLD, Wild Reckoning,* and *The Yale Review.*

Library of Congress Cataloging-in-Publication Data
Lasdun, James.
   [Poems. Selections]
   Bluestone : new and selected poems / James Lasdun. — First edition.
      pages ; cm
   ISBN 978-0-374-22055-6 (hardcover) —
   ISBN 978-0-374-53550-6 (softcover) —
   ISBN 978-0-374-71387-4 (ebook)
   I. Title.

PR6062.A735 A6 2015
821'.914—dc23

                                                              2014039380

Farrar, Straus and Giroux books may be purchased for educational, business, or promotional use. For information on bulk purchases, please contact the Macmillan Corporate and Premium Sales Department at 1-800-221-7945, extension 5442, or write to specialmarkets@macmillan.com.

www.fsgbooks.com
www.twitter.com/fsgbooks
www.facebook.com/fsgbooks

10 9 8 7 6 5 4 3 2 1

FOR ROBIN ROBERTSON

CONTENTS

A

JUMP

START

CELLO MUSIC

You're visiting a castle. There's a lake,
a hill, a wood, gardens, a herd of deer,
and then inside, paintings of lakes and hills,
mounted antlers, the cornucopian year
carved in four oak festoons—you're here to slake

a once-yearly thirst for the concentrate
of irretrievable times. It doesn't work—
like drinking to get drunk and staying sober;
the trees don't make a wood, that rain-pocked murk
won't turn into a lake, you can't translate

these stones into a castle . . . Later on,
reaching a village with a puddled street
and wet bronze soldier, slowing down, you see
framed in a window misted by the heat
of a single lamp and her own action,

a woman playing the cello, all alone
in a plain room at a plain brass music stand,
but cradling rose-grained curves and scrolls of wood
like something alive; one splayed-out, powerful hand
trembling where her blood pulses into the tone

as she plunges and draws back the bow.
She seems incongruous in this dead place,
its only light her own. You cannot hear
but you can see the music in her face,
tensing and letting go—you see it now

and it's not a face you see, but a lake
mottled like jade with lily pads, dead leaves,
goldfish scrolling silk-tailed through the black;
you climb a hill, and underfoot thick sheaves
of wet grass furrow silver like the track

a finger leaves in velvet. Browsing deer
move like a forest carpet come to life—
split chestnut eyes, bare branches, wet red leaves
dotted with melting snow, you catch a whiff
of wild rose, then white battlements appear.

SNAKE BURNING

Indolent creature, do you not observe
how the air is clotting with locusts? Coil
upon coil of you wreathes the dead acacia—
such heavy lumber to shift, such toil
to unravel yourself, each loop and curve . . .

I know that tired complexity, I too
would choose to think this heat the sun's alone.
Your tongue is mine, and we both taste burning
but lie as if our minds had turned to stone.
We could outsleep the limbs that cradle you.

Look now, the earth about you is alive:
plum-sized shrews, the golden field mice
and spark-bright lizards scuttle past your jaws.
A hare stumbles against you, butterflies
gyrate, the air is humming like a hive,

ground trembling beneath you, while overhead
in swift succession, deer and gazelle leap,
trailing their shadows across your body;
wisps of blue smoke arrive, and still you sleep . . .
What is it you and I cannot feel? Dread—

until the fury is upon us: fire
blazing in the grass, do you feel it now,
pooled in your contortions, furnacing?
You flex and writhe, but you have become slow
and each nerve seems to sing like a plucked wire.

I watch you dying; are we so alike
our deaths could be exchanged? I am entranced—
your last prey—watching your glazed marquetry
scorch, your body dance as it always danced,
your diamond head thrown back as if to strike.

THIS FEELING

At best the sparkle on the chain of being;
at worst an itch,
a superfetation,
the seconds-younger twin of sex,
resembling it as greed resembles hunger.

It was the cool of the evening,
the cruising hour;
shoals of eyes quivered pair on pair,
till a spark in the jelly blew the circuit.
You had to pitch yourself just above animal,

just below human—a tightrope
I wobbled on for three months;
Joe Allen's, The Closerie, Rose Bon-Bon,
gobbling on eyes, oysters, estrogen;
I was turning iridescent.

I came to my senses in a quayside bar—
an iris of purplish minnows round an ocher blob
bobbing on the water, then a dish
of the same but stiffened lustrous fry
set before me . . . I had to move.

It was one thing or the other—
dead air crammed with sweetnesses;
creams, effluvia streaming from the yachts,
winking oil-froth, a swarm
of sheeny girls on mopeds;

one of them landed ten yards from me;
I strolled up, a shambles of mime, and she
was off like a bluebottle,
publishing my disgrace
on a scroll of shimmering air . . .

THE TWO OF THEM

Their lives are turning into gold. The door
bristles with brass, its own commissionaire.
A valedictory hand swims up
through metal as I grasp it, then the glare
of summer spills like lacquer on the floor.

I step inside. A domed clock's pendulum
taps out a rally. Under glass, the spring
visibly unwinds. It's like a body
flayed open for its soul, where everything
but the invisible, heartbeat-beaten drum

of time itself is shown . . . Their rooms withhold
no secrets; I deduce the two of them
from every corner—even a window box,
the alchemist in the tulip stem
transmuting earth to shells of glassy gold.

They're in this sheen, from mornings when I'd watch
one of them brush the zodiacs of dust
from varnished wood, the yellow cotton's dark
reflection rising, brightening, till just
as it was turning into gold, the touch

of its own substance snuffed it out . . . Sometimes
I find them in the garden, gin in hand,
the fizz still showering upward through the glass,
while insects brush their skin like sprinkled sand
and lazy fingers spin a bowl of limes.

Summer evenings . . . Silence like a sheet
pockmarked by a sound beyond the wall,
from the tennis courts, and once or twice a night,
out of the blue, a Day-Glo tennis ball
sails over, bounces round our feet

and skitters on, almost as if in fun,
idling to a halt at someone's chair,
and then it's like a chill, and I imagine
arriving to discover no one here,
the two of them now one of them, now none.

ABOVE LAGGAN

Low sun, low mist, long shadows probe the water,
wild cotton flares in the contracting dusk,
the harebells flex to voltage in the stalk
and wheat germ stiffens in its husk;
down on the fallow field the rabbits scatter
maddened by the shadow of a hawk.

Whoever looks desires that quickening death;
to flare like matchlight, stiffen, flex or run,
somehow to evade the supernumerary,
to have one's shadow lengthened by the sun
and hold, elect, one's tenantry of earth
whereof all things are but a colonie . . .

You could lie here imagining chance might fall
from nowhere, like a hawk, or that the wind,
to whose calligraphy the hill-grass yields,
might write as vividly across the mind,
leaving indelible the kestrel's call,
cloud-shadow spreading stains across the fields.

VANISHING POINTS

Earth in her own shadow like a cat in heat
lures down the gods; you catch a musk,
the brandied scent of Sekhmet on the frost,
a whiff of naphtha in the lamp-bronzed dusk,
iced gutters crackling underfoot.

Body warm in its coat, soul in body
snug as a whetted dagger in its sheath,
you smile the parenthetical smile
of a terminal case
and mark the mineral springtime of a city—

these shuttered market stalls, a tethered cart,
booths locked and bolted—budded morning's fleece
of cut-price watches, calculators, rugs—
the everlasting bloom . . . bliss can be peace,
or tumult, an anvil's clamor in the heart

as when a line takes shape inside the mind;
set sail, the wind is fair, the ocean taut,
this is the rare, the protozoic moment,
moistened for the corkscrew bolt of thought
to lay its flashburn signature, and wind

the world about its helix: finished things
come swiftly into words, where seconds past
they stood in the abstract language of the earth—
a meter's totem skull, the plane trees' vast
dark cumulus of leaves, and glimmerings,

vanishing points, an idea melting out
like sleet on skin, like the brain in its brief state
between death and dissolution, when it keels—
Atlantis in the flood-tide spate,
the frescoes fading on its walls, a shout

echoing through the galleries . . . or days
dull as a lover's past; days when a song
you thought came out that year was after all
a decade old: recall them now, the long
hot afternoons, time sticky in its glaze

of too much humid sky; days when you'd watch
the widow from the basement stand
hours on end in the public phone
chattering, while her eloquent hand
bunched up, as if it didn't matter much

that the line was dead; oh bright scintillae,
photons, gravitons, the hidden shirr
of substance; final, indivisible
iotas that must move or disappear—
recessions of light that leave a human body

thin as a shadow, spectral, feather-blown,
spinning among the self's unlit cortege
of ghost selves aching for the something lost
when mirrors leave a room, or tilt a wedge
of mountainside, and flip it upside down . . .

Meths, white spirit, petrol, polish—smells
that led you upward like a spiral stair,
leaving you reeling in the vaporized
ice-bright striations of a sky, the glare
of shattered sunlight on the pitching swells

of a distant sea, its yellow shoreline
darkened by gliding shadow-clouds, or by
the sliding bridal trains of draining waves—
somewhere a disturbance, a harsh human cry,
and one man less climbs out than waded in.

WOMAN

POLICE

OFFICER

IN

ELEVATOR

THE CALLING OF THE
APOSTLE MATTHEW

Not the abrupt way, frozen
in the one glance of a painter's frame,
Christ in the doorway pointing, Matthew's face
bright with perplexity, the glaze
of a lifetime at the countinghouse
cracked in the split second's bolt of being chosen,

but over the years, slowly,
hinted at, an invisible curve;
persistent bias always favoring
backwardly the relinquished thing
over the kept, the gold signet ring
dropped in a beggar's bowl, the eye not fully

comprehending the hand, not yet;
heirloom damask thrust in a passing
stranger's hand, the ceremonial saddle
(looped coins, crushed clouds of inlaid pearl)
given on an irresistible
impulse to a servant. Where it sat,

a saddle-shaped emptiness
briefly, obscurely brimming . . . Flagons,
cellars of wine, then as impulse steadied
into habit, habit to need,
need to compulsion, the whole vineyard,
the land itself, groves, herds, the ancestral house

given away, each object's
hollowed-out void successively
more vivid in him than the thing itself,
as if renouncing merely gave
density to having; as if
he'd glimpsed in nothingness a derelict's

secret of unabated,
inverse possession . . . And only then,
almost superfluous, does the figure
step softly to the shelter door;
casual, foreknown, almost familiar,
calmly received, like someone long awaited.

WOMAN POLICE OFFICER IN ELEVATOR

Not that I'd ever noticed
either a taste or a distaste
for that supposedly arousing
rebus of pain and desire, the uniformed woman,
whether as Dietrich in epaulettes,
or armored like Penthesileia, or in thigh boots
and cocked hat, straddling the Atlantic,
fishing for campesinos
with live torpedoes,

but when the rattling, john-sized
tenement elevator paused
mid-fall to blink a female housing cop
into its humid cranium, I felt her presence
spooling through me like a Mobius strip,
splicing her spilling curls, nightstick, the gun at her hip,
chrome shield, the breast it emblazoned,
seamlessly into the same
restless continuum . . .

I caught—was it possible?—
the scent of some sweet-tinctured oil;
troubling, arousing, and looked away

then glanced back obliquely: had I imagined it,
that sudden scimitar-glint of danger,
or had some forbidden impulse—longing, lust, anger—
tumid inside me like a hidden
semiautomatic
in a schoolkid's lunchpack

triggered the blue-lashed, tiny
metal detector of her eye?
I backed against my corner, watching
the numerals slowly swallow their green gulp of light;
interminable! And as we fell,
our little locked cube of stale air seemed to bristle
with a strange menace . . . I thought of harms;
my own and not my own,
contemplated or done;

betrayals, infidelities,
coercions, seductions, lies,
ready to confess them all and more,
as if in her firm indifference she'd regressed me
inward down some atavistic line
to the original essence, the masculine
criminal salt; a frieze of victims
paneled in my own skull
like a lit cathedral hell . . .

A shudder, and then stillness;
avoidance of each other's eyes
as in some bedroom fiasco's wake,
the air too brimful with disclosure, till the door
opened and we parted, the clamped rift
between us widening like a continental drift
of the sexes; she to the butcher, the breaker,
the ripper, the rapist,
I to my therapist.

THE REVENANT

Jetlag, a jumpcut dawn, distempered
daze of brickdust and rosedust,
ache of memory, insomniac mumble of June;
the worst of absence is return,
already not becoming what you once

almost already were . . . Forgotten things
forget themselves; the spellbound mirrors slumber
dreaming of sand. A shut book dreams of lumber.
You wake them once a year,
every year it gets harder.

Delicate hour,
mica, translucent moon,
hue of penitence (sham) on sleeping windows;
you walk to the borough gardens:
locked, but a demolished house leads through,

and you stand in the exfoliated green of your own past,
between the pond and the bench where the blind men sat;
chestnuts plowing the light—domed emerald rubble—
and a rain of birdsong gibbering like a language
you no longer speak or understand.

LIME PICKLE

Your father, not yet divorced,
rosy-cheeked from the Garrick
in his Savile Row pin-striped suit,
presided over the feast.

He spread the menu like a general's map,
plotting his debauch
on the virginal palates
of his teenage daughter and her first "chap."

In our singular innocence
we had tasted nothing stronger
or stranger than each other's lips,
but your father's extravagance

(it broke him later)
shoaling in salvers on the table
under the tabla's gulp and throb,
and the moan of a sitar

made our mouths water.
Unlidded, the dishes sizzled;
spiced, cream-rich, sprinkled with edible gold;
a taste of our imminent future,

though what I recall
most clearly twenty years on
as I read his obit in *The Times*,
is the spoonful of lime pickle

he tricked me into eating;
his harsh laughter
as it burned like a living coal
on my astounded tongue

which however has learned
his own preference for mixed blessings,
having grown sharper since then,
and thicker-skinned.

LANDSCAPE WITH
BUBBLES AND BROOM

I watch the bubbles pearling on the ice
of an early morning *spremúto*. As I drink,
the swaying ice cubes click and clink
and shower the fanlight of a lemonslice
with a fine silvery seethe of air.
My palate tingles. My head begins to clear . . .

Outside it's sunny. A sundial cypress
vogues against the Tuscan stubble's
cloth of gold. Hot-air balloons like bubbles
bulge from the earth . . . Inside, a T V hostess
shimmies in lamé on a kitsch
soccer theme-set . . . Apropos of which

you could have heard a pin drop
on the hotel lobby's salami-of-marble tile
when Baggio's ball sailed skyward and Brazil
lobbed in the winner. Only the wry pop
of a champagne cork reminded us defeat
was somehow more . . . Italian. All night

footballs bobbed in my dreams, and now I think
of bubbles again. Bubbles! The very word
almost unsayably absurd;
its own brief globed and breaking blink,
foaming a lightness through my own
inclination to be stone . . .

Undust, unatom, matter's vowel,
paradigm for the self-invented joke
sidewinding out of its teller . . . Zero's cloak,
mirror and ally of all things possible . . .
Now the balloons slide up. Their climb unlocks
the valley's *Wünderkammer*, its treasure box:

level on level of dovetailed slopes
tumbling downward like the imprint
of a vast pontifical pinecone; squint
vineyards, olive groves, orchards; a hand-hewn landscape's
novelistic casual-but-cunning detail;
everything plotted, fitted into its petal-

garden- or meadow-shaped slot of space
just so,
and the sensational yellow
broomflower banners wheeling down every crevice
as if the land were swiveling in gold light
or popping with sprinkled dynamite

or gilding itself for Guidoriccio's steed
to ride again . . . For surely a place must *want*
this added brilliance to let it run so rampant;
Christ, even the birds are crested;
little heralds, the local bugle call—
"all for glory, and enough glory for all"

or possibly "*Forza Italia!*" given
how for the third time the lictor's rods
have ousted the bucolic local gods—
rings in your ears all day . . .
                              Now on the screen
the hostess *spanks* the ball for being bad.
It looks like something out of Kierkegaard;

mankind "astray in possibility,"
begging the question—that lamé swimsuit:
is that what happens when a jackboot
pupates: its billowing butterfly?
Is *sprezzatura* merely "flatulent knowledge"?
No longer the fructifying pledge

of the six red balls
dancing on the Medici crest?
And Lightness: the milky marble breast
of Pisano's virgin, or Berlusconi's belles
so pumped you half expect the screens to rise
like iridescent bubbles before your eyes?

Is there a difference? I drain my glass;
the used ice rustles: a fishlike, flat
ghost of itself. The juice is also flat.
It needs its little spritz of nothingness
to give it life. Hence, doubtless, heaven
likened in the gospels unto leaven

"hid in three measures of meal . . ."
Hence the sculptor's taste for marble's
air- and light-loving calcite bubbles.
Hence the doctor's rod of sharpened steel
for plunging in your lung when it collapses.
Hence also the poet's weakness for ellipses . . .

I step outside. The broomflower's soapy smell
drifts on the breeze . . . Hard not to feel a strange
volatile happiness here, as if a change
of shape were always imminent; that sparkle
of salt-light on the sky's crushed lapis dome
Venus perpetually rising from the foam . . .

POWDER COMPACT

Twenties, machine-age cloisonné, steel lines
curving through the enamel plaque;
priced voluptuously—as I wrote the check
my new love surged on its own extravagance . . .
Nocturnal, businesslike, here was your brisk
sinuous walk, your pagan/Puritan air;
it was like buying you in miniature . . .
I didn't look inside. A stifling musk
burst on us as you opened it: the past;
the original owner's scented powder puff.
That's all. I didn't catch *memento mori*
whispered in her spilt, too intimate dust
till now, or read in hers, love's epitaph,
still pink and scut-soft in its reliquary.

TIMING

The secret of good comedy. Ours was bad,
a hothouse passion blooming under force
of imminent separation. Were our eyes
bigger than our hearts? A candlebud
of amaryllis burned for you in my room
three thousand miles away. You stalled your visit
twice, mysteriously, and came too late.
Our out-of-sync phone calls were a bad dream—
echolocation of love . . . My lopped bromeliad's
adze-stumps turned to black bronze as you rode
the planet into light, five hours ahead.
Even when you came we lived in shifts,
watching the amaryllis's oxblood explode;
ten days of brilliance, then abruptly dead.

AFTERNOON LETTER

Back, and as if a spell
had broken, I could almost
bring myself to open what I'd closed
for seven years; your image, vector
of disappointments, and speak in the tone of the shriven.
So in that deep street's swiftly decanting dazzle
I fell in step with our seven years' younger selves
and like an objective ghost

saw us for what we were,
which was to say more or less
as others, each other's best but wrong guess.
This was our quarter: butcher, *fabbro*,
this was our doorway; impregnable, seven years thick,
behind it our dark flat with its summer furniture,
brick alcove I stood in forming words you watched me
almost utter then suppress.

Others are in there now.
It gives itself to their lives,
offers them in its eaves and alcoves
substance tractable to memory;

says: "for this contentment, boredom, sadness,
here is an afternoon silence, out there a *fabbro*,
his can of smoking varnish, his bullshorn anvil,
there the lanceolate leaves

of an oleander;
assume this contingency
into your days here as the tree
drinks from beneath these salmon-scale cobbles
its globe of shivering leaves . . ." Bells rang, the day was passing,
crying in tongues: *One life only to transfigure*,
and as if I'd switched sides in a train
and what once rushed to meet me

started slipping away,
I felt wrenched forward, estranged,
while everything—street, sky, you—seemed plunged
in valedictory shadow; old photographs
of faces in which a posthumous knowledge
had worked a premonitory sorrow in each eye,
an almost visible change of expression . . .
Otherwise nothing had changed.

ZOPILOTES

Between two villages where the rows
of agave thin to a scrub of crabgrass
and red clay slung like a gaunt pelt
over a pelvis of rocks; beside a road
melting out into oiled air either end,
the body of a horse lies where it fell
in a rigging of entrails; plundered skull
bleaching to socketed chalk. A vulture,
caged like a black heart in its tattered hull,
eases her neck out between two ribs,
twists and croaks skyward where her mate
wheels in the blue. Before he drops
she steps from the belly, preens her ruff and chooses,
assiduously, a gobbet of flesh, then hops
onto the wobbling carcass, and as he lands
jabs it into his mouth. And there,
on a bed of carrion with clattering bones for springs,
in a studious rapture, as if intent
on probing the outer dustward limits of flesh,
they couple—two scorched angels; connoisseurs
of fallenness; apostate saints of love,
fanning a black-flamed blaze with their beating wings.

THE COURTESAN

After Rilke

Venice; alchemical daylight
touches my hair: a lock of sunstruck gold.
My eyebrows arch like her bridges. Look:
under their angled shadows runs the cold
glitter of my eyes; canals
quietly trafficking while the sea
ebbs and surges inside them, a brimming
blue-green dilation . . . Whoever looks at me
envies my lapdog on whose pampered coat,
distractedly, I sometimes rest a hand,
jeweled, invulnerable, white as my own throat . . .
Nighttime finds my chambers manned
by our illustrious families' cherished youth
who drop as if by poison at my mouth.

PLAGUE YEARS

"There is, it would seem, in the dimensional scale of
the world, a kind of delicate meeting place between
imagination and knowledge, a point, arrived at by
diminishing large things and enlarging small ones, that is
intrinsically artistic." —Vladimir Nabokov, *Speak, Memory*

Sore throat, persistent cough . . . The campus doctor
tells me "just to be safe" to take the test.
The clinic protocol seems to insist
on an ironic calm. I hold my fear.
He draws a vial of blood for the City Lab,
I have to take it there, but first I teach
a class on Nabokov. Midway I reach
into my bag for *Speak, Memory* and grab
the hot bright vial instead. I seem at once
wrenched from the quizzical faces of my class
into some silent anteroom of hell:
the "delicate meeting place," I feel it pounce;
terror—my life impacted in the glass,
my death enormous in its scarlet grail.

ERYSICHTHON

After Ovid

I

The scene: a town under mountains;
clapboard, shingle and brick, the usual
straggle of shopping malls, post-colonial
factory outlets and fast-food chains
thinning upward through scant
cattle pastures then woods
where the hulk of a disused chemical plant

drips and leaks. This was built by one
Erysichthon, who as it happens
also built the malls and fast-food chains,
outlets too—in fact who'd built the town,
downtown at least; who owned
a piece of everything,
and several pieces of the board who'd zoned

or rather rezoned certain lands
once listed "Grade A Conservation"
as "Grade E, suitable for speculation,"

placing in their benefactor's hands
the local beauty spots
which he, magician-like,
tore to pieces and turned into parking lots,

malls, outlets, chains, etcetera.
This is our hero, Erysichthon;
ex-boxer, self-styled entrepreneur, ex-con
(wire fraud, two years in a white-collar
"country club"), after which
the town received him back
with open arms. Why not? He'd made them rich,

some of them anyway, besides
he had a certain big man's swagger
people admire; a cross between an ogre
and Father Christmas: three hundred pounds,
bearded, built like a vat,
with a great booming voice
and a cuff on the chin that could knock you flat.

He and his daughter, a shy girl
who doted on him in a perverse
return for his neglect, abuse or worse,
lived in a ramshackle Gothic pile
with its own pool and grounds,
planned by himself, put up
by his own men, and just as he cheated friends,

so he'd managed to cheat himself:
cheap timbers warping, shoddy brickwork
damp on the plastered insides, outside a murk
of crooked-lined mortar; not a shelf,
door or cupboard nailed straight,
the skimped-on pipes bursting
every winter . . . Yet over this second-rate

botched-up construction seemed to float
a yearning, an almost palpable
dream of grandeur and splendor, of epic scale—
vintage cars in the drive, a powerboat
dry-docked in the garage,
barbecues big enough
for hogs and oxes on the tilting acreage

of the rear porch: pure appetite
so strong at first glance it seemed to change
will into deed, so that briefly by a strange
hypnotism you transformed the sight
into its own ideal,
pinnacled, shimmering,
as if he'd tripped you up on some hidden zeal

you yourself harbored for excess . . .
This was his secret; to sell his clients
on their own luck-rich dreams. The plant for instance

(electrolyte for capacitors)—
he'd lured the company
less by the usual talk
of tax breaks, kickbacks, etcetera, than by

some potent, invisible
spume of unlimited confidence
that reached them from his squat bulk like the hormones
by which certain animals compel
others to roll over
and get shafted, which was
precisely what they did. Within a year

the concrete floor had fissured. Waste
seeped through the cracks. Teratogenic
(lit.: "monster-breeding") PCBs and toxic
potions to suit every other taste
were found in a nearby
spring-fed pool where hunters
told of seeing at twilight an unearthly

fluorescence in the reeds, of strange
deformities in local creatures:
web-footed mice, snakes with fur in patches,
dropped antlers with a bluish mineral tinge . . .
True or not, the place shut
and for a while our man
was banned from the trade. But genius will out,

and in his retreat from the world
(this was how he preferred to term it)
he had a vision, as befits a hermit:
before him a spread of trees unfurled—
a radiant, flower-filled wood
with a clearing in which
clusters of brand-new sun-shot houses stood.

Luxury homes; but more than just
luxurious (and this is what we mean
by genius); he'd design the whole thing green!
What? Erysichthon turned ecologist?
Apparently. No scam
surely could bring such pious
tears to his eyes; "I'm green, I really am,"

he said out loud as a swell
of righteousness filled his heart: "I'll build
windmills and solar panels, use recycled
paper for prospectuses and sell
not houses but ideals
carved in organic forms
from eco-friendly natural materials . . . ,

let's say a million bucks apiece
which isn't much considering
how good you'll feel just living there and saving

the earth, in fact it's cheap at the price."
So to the zoning board
whose members could be seen
later that year at choice resorts abroad

sunning themselves, expenses paid.
Then to the S&L, a boardroom lunch
to pitch for funds: "My friends, I have a hunch
that one day on our children's lips Cascade"
(his name for the project)
"will be a word for hope;
a word for how we didn't self-destruct,

a word for courage, for the best
in our great nation under God, the true
spirit of enterprise, get-up-and-go, can-do.
Call me a bleeding heart, an idealist,
call me a renegade
liberal, but my friends
I have a hunch that history wants Cascade;

I have a hunch that one day we
who built it will have built a paradise
sung with our fruited plains and spacious skies,
praised with our purple mountains' majesty . . ."
And so on till the air
filled with directors' sobs.
"We're in," they cried, "we're green, we really are."

II

High above town a first-growth wood
fanned out from a crease in the mountain
where waterfalls churned a mist like pile-driven
marble dust; a sparkling quarry cloud
on which a rainbow played.
This was the lucky site
our hero had selected for Cascade,

though to a certain sect in town,
keepers of a certain mystic flame,
the wood had long been known by another name:
the White and Blue. In spring the waving crown
of dogwood and hawthorn trees
formed a white cumulus
of blossom above, while like a tapestry's

millefleur background, an undergrowth
of cream-colored wildflowers spread below—
featherbells, sweet white violets, moonseed, yarrow,
trembling wood anemones—till the earth
foamed like a breaking wave
with living surf. And then,
as spring passed, blue, the blue of a chapel nave

under a blue rose window rose
like a blue-blooded blush into the white;

wild hyacinth, hyssop skullcap, aconite,
blooming over the ground while buckthorn sloes
and juniper berries
hung ripening above.
Here our sect, a sisterhood of Ceres—

white witches mostly—assorted
healers, herbalists and hierophants
of Wicca—came each month to gather plants:
cohosh, lobelia roots, enchanter's nightshade,
white milkweed for the heart,
emetic gentian, raw
matter for every magic or mystic art.

Needless to say the White and Blue
was precious to them, and when the word
of Cascade reached their ears, they flew to the wood,
arriving just as Erysichthon's crew
were unloading chainsaws.
Circling a central stand
of ancient trees they cried: "This wood is ours,

sacred to our goddess. Touch it
and our curse be on your heads." The crew
hung back: in this uncertain era few
had quite the rashness not to admit
at least a vague belief
in most things spiritual—
curses, auras, Atlantis, an afterlife

on other planets; however,
our hero, drunk on his rhetoric,
had lathered up an almost messianic
zeal for his project, and a quiver
of indignation shook
his great bulk as he learned
of this pious protest. Jumping in his truck

and barreling up to the wood,
where he found the women hand in hand
stalling his men, he bellowed: "This is my land,
let me get at those trees or you're as good
as lumber yourselves. I paid"
(grabbing a chainsaw here)
"my money, now I've come to build Cascade."

And holding out the saw, he strode
towards the protestors. One of them,
a gray-haired, soft-spoken woman by the name
of Gendenwitha (Iroquois word
for Day Star), gently stepped
out of the ring and spoke
of her own ancestors who'd worshipped

in this very spot; of how each
tree was once thought to contain a soul
"So that to chop—" But with a contemptuous snarl

Erysichthon cut her off mid-speech,
giving the starter cord
of his chainsaw a yank,
and revving the engine till the big blade roared

violently into life; and so,
wielding it wildly in front of him,
he cut through an iron-hard hornbeam, lopped each limb
of an oak from its trunk, and as though
the mutilated stump
woke some demon in him,
he rampaged through the wood; slashed out at a clump

of hazels that leapt like soldiers
blown from a trench . . . Pines and birches fell
under the swipe of his blade, a sour smell
of sap rose into the air, loud cries
from the scattered women
running from tree to tree
vied with the chainsaw roar, and seemed to madden

their enemy into a state
of apoplectic outrage . . . Up ahead
he saw a great blossoming tree, a dogwood
held by some to house the wood's own spirit.
Gashing it with his blade
he sprang back in surprise:
out of the wood poured sap the color of blood:

a scarlet banner unfurling
into the White and Blue . . . and then the tall
glittering dome of the tree began to fall;
twisting, the leaves and blossoms swirling,
trunk splintering like a bone,
and as it crashed, the whole
wood and hillside echoed with the groan.

III

Meanwhile Gendenwitha came
to the waterfall, where on her knees
she prayed out loud: "Demeter, Ishtar, Ceres,
Papothkwe (to use my people's name)—
life force of every plant;
you whose reality
we've honored to this day in blind faith, grant

some token of yourself, and if
our love can't bring you into being
then let this man's brutality." So saying,
she looked up at the foam-curtained cliff
and in the rainbow glaze
saw suddenly the bright
voluptuous shimmering figure of the goddess.

Trembling, dazzled, she heard a voice
close in her ear like a rush of wind
whisper, "Daughter, follow this stream till you find
a cinder-block shack. This is the House
of Hunger. Go inside,
tell Hunger to visit
Erysichthon." With which the vision faded.

So the woman set out along
the twisting stream that led through the wood
where its pure waters took on a tint of blood
from the sacred tree. From there the long
fall past fields and quarries,
cities, suburbs, thruways,
stockyards and junkyards, strip mines, foundries, factories,

added a number of other
interesting tints to the stream—spilt oil,
solvents, pesticides, slurries, lead—until
nothing was left for Gendenwitha
to follow but a thin
ooze of mud-colored sludge
that crawled across a desolate moonlike plain

of exhausted farmland; barren,
skeletal orchards, rusting silos,
dry irrigation pipes crisscrossing meadows

of dust, with here and there a warren
of crooked-chimneyed huts,
slumped trailers where old cars
sank in the mud out front, and starving mutts

skulked by trash cans; till at last
a little cinder-block shack appeared:
doorless, derelict-looking . . . The woman peered
into the shadows. There in the dust
sat a hollow-eyed child
dressed in rags, neglected;
over her wizened, listess face hung soiled

clumps of thin hair; her lips were cracked,
sores crusted her throat, her brittle bones
stuck out under her scooped-out shoulders and loins,
and long claws seemed to have gouged the racked
furrows in her rib cage.
This was Hunger. A spoon
dangled from her hand, and a look of reproach,

ancient and unappeasable,
glistened in her eyes. Without a word
she listened to Ceres' commands and followed
the woman back up the stream until
they reached the road that led
to Erysichthon's house.
Night had fallen. The great man lay in bed

Snoring too loud to hear his door
creak open and Hunger slip inside.
Climbing onto the bed, she squatted astride
his chest, then down through his gaping jaw
inserted her long spoon
and in one deft movement
emptied him out, then pressed his lips with her own,

breathing herself into his blood
till famine blazed there . . . Then out she crept
back to her hovel. As Erysichthon slept
he started dreaming vividly of food:
hunks of succulent meat
in pungent sauces, pies,
pastries, ripe cheeses; raising a forkful to eat

he ground his teeth on air, and woke
with a strange fierce hunger in his guts . . .
Down at the fridge he rummaged for cold cuts,
then called his daughter and had her cook
a breakfast of waffles,
home fries, bacon and eggs,
and wolfed it down. Within an hour or less

he was hungry again, and called
for another breakfast—"And this time
don't skimp on me. Let's see, we'll start with a prime
rib of Black Angus, then a nice grilled

turkey and swiss on rye,
then I think apple cake
with maple whipped cream . . . no, make that pecan pie,

or both in fact." The girl obeyed.
He gulped down the meal, went off to work
up at Cascade with his men, where hunger struck
once again with a pang that made
his flesh pour sweat like wax
from a melting candle:
so about-turn, stopping off for Big Macs

and cheese steaks . . . Back at home he ordered
his dumbstruck daughter to cook him up
"something substantial. None of this diet crap.
Give me some corned beef hash, some breaded
pork chops. I want meat loaf,
donuts and marshmallows.
Bake me some shrimp . . . Don't stand there gaping. Move!"

So it continued, day and night;
daughter cooking while her father ate,
breaking off only to breathe and defecate,
then only to breathe: his appetite
was such that he was soon
obliged to take his meals
(or rather his one endless meal) on the throne,

where like an upturned alchemist
he steadily turned his gold to shit:
cash, vintage cars, then the yacht, then bit by bit
the land, the house itself, till the last
dollar slid down the drain
and he and his daughter
found themselves abruptly out in the rain

without a penny. What to do?
Beg on street corners? The nickels fell
like a few useless waterdrops in hell
on the flames of his appetite, which grew
livelier and hotter
every minute till sheer
pain brought inspiration: "I'll sell my daughter!"

So for ten bucks he pimped the child
there on the street (this touching detail
is taken straight from Ovid's original
just in case the reader thinks we've piled
it on a bit too thick);
but while the girl was gone
a sudden pang of hunger like a mule kick

stabbed his belly . . . He had to eat
something, anything, without delay:
smashing a butcher's window, he grabbed a tray

of sirloin slabs and fled down the street
tearing off lumps of steak
with his teeth as he ran
up out of town to the woods, where like a shark

in a feeding frenzy, he lost
all distinction between what was food
and what was his living flesh: with a jagged
blade of slate he hacked a plump red roast
from his own arm; the bone
soon glistened white, stripped bare;
and just as he'd mauled the trees, he mauled his own

limbs and trunk in a consuming
fury of hunger and pain until
he'd eaten half his body. A certain pool,
mentioned before, lay quietly fuming
in the damp air close by:
here, as Erysichthon
staggered onward, reeling from tree to tree

deranged, blood-spattered like a bear
savaged by wolves—himself both victim
and pack of predators tearing at each limb—
he paused, and lapped the potent water,
then limped off upward, drawn
by a stumbling instinct
back to the scene of his desecration.

A sewage ditch now crossed the bulldozed
building site: he tumbled in, and here
his mutilated shape began to alter
into its own double-orificed
essence of greed and waste;
mouth and rear end opening
to two huge O's; stomach and barrel chest

hollowing out from rim to rim,
hardening as his limbs disappeared
and nothing was left of him but a yard
of concrete pipe. And there we leave him,
soon to be delivered
from his own emptiness
forever, or at least until the wood

reclaims Cascade.
                    Meanwhile beyond
much remains still to be spoiled: in fall
hillsides still assemble their unsaleable
red and yellow mosaic; on every pond
floats the same old mottled
surrealist carpet; green
globes of foliage dip themselves in gold

for no discernible purpose.
Then come dustier colors; ochers,
tawny oranges, browns of bracts and burrs,

bristly asters, leafless trees like patches
of worn plush in a once
sumptuous court's faded
velvet upholstery, where skeletons

gemmed with crab apples breathe a sour
musk of cider . . . Then winter arrives:
pathos of molting angels, arthritic leaves
gloved by hissing snow that in an hour
fashions a scrupulous
translation of each tree
into a bright new language, and then blows

its work to pieces, as doubtless
every translator should. Then springtime's
mint of glinting foliage—a billion dimes—
tumbles out of dry twigs; superfluous
miracle we cherish
each year more anxiously
as if the very notion of a fresh

beginning has begun to fray
and seem implausible; as if
against life's optimistic faith in life
too much evidence has come to weigh,
and almost everything
it liked about itself
suddenly seems autumnal, even spring.

LANDSCAPE

WITH

CHAINSAW

LOCALS

They peopled landscapes casually like trees,
being there richly, never having gone there,
and whether clanning in cities or village-thin stands
were reticent as trees with those not born there,
and their fate, like trees, was seldom in their hands.

Others to them were always one of two
evils: the colonist or refugee.
They stared back, half disdaining us, half fearing;
inferring from our looks their destiny
as preservation or as clearing.

I envied them. To be local was to know
which team to support: the local team;
where to drop in for a pint with mates: the local;
best of all to feel by birthright welcome
anywhere; be everywhere a local . . .

Bedouin-Brython-Algonquins; always there
before you; the original prior claim
that made your being anywhere intrusive.
There, doubtless, in Eden before Adam
wiped them out and settled in with Eve.

Whether at home or away, whether kids
playing or saying what they wanted,
or adults chatting, waiting for a bus,
or, in their well-tended graves, the contented dead,
there were always locals, and they were never us.

AMERICAN MOUNTAIN

I

Our Queen's English accents
kept the class-conscious English masses
at bay, while our looks and name
did the same for the upper classes.

Being there,
as opposed to just stopping by,
was a matter of what you arrived too late
to arrange: your ancestry.

"We're not English" went the family saying.
What were we then? We'd lopped
our branch off from the family tree:
anglophone Russian-German apostate Jews

mouthing Anglican hymns at church
till we renounced that too . . . Self-knowledge
was knowledge of not being this or this or this.
We were like stencils: our inverse had the edge

over whatever it was we were,
not that that would have mattered had I not
happened not to enjoy that throttling
knot of annulled speech gathering in my throat,

or the sense of not being in a room
I hadn't left, or being too light
to plant my feet. I was my opposite;
I chased myself across the planet

till I vanished through the looking glass
of the Atlantic Ocean
and woke up clinging to the tilted
patchwork of an American mountain.

II A FAMILY TREE

The locals,
Esopus Algonquins,
having already been massacred,
there's no one with greater claim to an acre

than you have. As for your ancestry, it's yours
to choose from whoever cleared a spot
anywhere on these tough-fibered slopes and hollows.
Patent your own coat of arms—why not?

Elect your forebears from the pitch-brewers,
colliers, tanbark-peelers, the German
smelters at DeZeng's forge hammering molten
pigs of primordial bog-iron; shingle-splitters,

Dutch buckwheat farmers
who felled a white pine to pitch their claim,
cleared the land, then when the tree
rotted, had them a home;

apostate royalists who took "The Test";
I have it by heart: *I the Subscriber*
do most solemnly swear
that I renounce all allegiance to the King of Great Britain . . .

Take your pick, you'll know them
by what they left behind—
great bluestone dolmens the Irish quarrymen
cut and hauled down ice roads, then abandoned;

abandoned orchards from Prohibition
when a backwoodsman could stay afloat
on twenty barrels of hard cider,
his knobbled trees still cranking out squint fruit;

abandoned houses—middle-income,
cathedral-ceilinged, faux post-and-beam
"Woodstock Contemporaries"
dotted along the creeks for IBM

before they downsized; abandoned gristmills, graveyards
(and what landscape isn't finally the sum
of others' abandoned efforts to turn it
into themselves? Only the too tame

or the impossibly wild . . .).
As for my own family tree, I'd gladly
grandfather-in our predecessors
here on this slope of the mountain: glassblowers,

Bohemians mostly, shipped over
between the Embargo boom and the peacetime crash
—a brief, bright window—
to couple the virgin forests of Keefe Hollow

with the sands of Cooper Lake.
I see them at the glory hole
in their leather aprons and masks,
emptying their strong lungs

into the shimmering lungs of glass . . .
Choristers, fiddlers, jugglers,
with a taste for the gaudy,
they left behind almost nothing—

a few glass whimsies: dippers, turtles and canes;
bits of glass slag gleaming in the dirt,
and a marginal local
increase in transparency.

Lichtung: a clearing;
firebreak or beaver meadow,
Dutch farmer-pioneer meadows, stump-littered and raw;
first harvest ashes; second, Indian corn
tilled with a thornbush harrow.

"A man was famous,"
the psalm reports, "according
as he had lifted up axes upon thick trees."
The trees are still thick, and although you've traded
that king for the secret king

of thought, and exchanged
your axe for a Makita,
it remains a matter of the ground beneath you; first
making it *unverborgen*: unconcealed,
then second, planting your feet.

I've muddled it all
like the old-time dairymen
in their doggerel of gable and saltbox, their pastures
a garble of ditches. But that's how it is
after *Verfall*. The fallen

tend to a certain
makeshift approach towards life.

Like Kant they know nothing straight has ever been built
from the crooked timber of humanity,
and just keep patching the roof.

Theirs is the kingdom
of God, or at any rate
Dasein. Being here's just a question of having been
elsewhere unhappily long enough to feel
that that was exile, this not.

ADAM

Seed-hoarder: tipping his paper pouches
in unnibbleable coffers; fencing,
filching our food, homeland; won't chatter
the local woods brogue of chirrup and chuck,
his othering tongue unchristening tree,
unrocking rock.

He's not one of us; he's
definitely not one of us:
unstriped meat-breather pissing ammonia; we feign
blitheness but from each
brush-pile, oak-stump, ash-limb,
we are watching him.

EVE

I like that room,
the warm one with the machines
where the woman folds her shed skins.

I hang in the broken ceiling, watching her,
barely distinguishable
from the cold water pipe
and the coiled power cable.

I watch her all winter:
her long-legged hands,
the glinting needles of fur at her nape,
her red warmness
drifting in mammaly billows.

And now I show myself;
pour my flickering head
into her sac of air,
and slowly, willed against her own will,
her face rises like a rising moon,
opening palely to mine,

and in the wide O's of her eyes,
I see myself: my head like a big cut jewel,
the little watch-jewels of my eyes, yes,
my tongue the alive nerve of a rock,
and I feel her want,
a yearning almost,
as though for something already about to be lost,

and I offer myself.

RETURNING THE GIFT

For Nicholas Jenkins

For my birthday
my wife gives me a chainsaw;
a shiny blue Makita,
big as our child, heavy

as an impacted planet.
On every part of its body the makers
have slapped red warning stickers:
Stop! Danger of Death! Do Not Operate

Unless Experienced! The manual
elaborates: kickback,
where the blade bucks back through your neck;
blinding by woodchip or exploding fuel,

death by misguided tree-fall, tissue necrosis
from the engine vibrations . . . I look at my wife,
wondering what it means for a woman to give
her husband a gift such as this . . .

You said we needed one, remember?
She smiles, and it's true;
we're losing our meadow
to red maple, alder, poplar.

But the warnings . . . **Do Not Operate
Unless Experienced!** . . . For two weeks
I leave it untouched in its box,
then when I take it out,

a feeling of fear sinks through me:
must I deliberately rouse this murderous gift,
cradle its killing shaft
between my soft arms and belly,

carry it up where the old dairy pasture begins,
where the poplars loom sixty feet tall
with a sixty-foot will not to fall,
and plunge it into their skins?

*

Strip-mall country: the chain
molecule of a shingled cinder-block cube
polymerized into HoJo's, Jiffy Lube,
Walmart, Kmart and—where we're headed—Miron:

Museum of the American Present,
where can-do meets do-it-yourself,
where you can grab a dump truck off the shelf
or a family-sized nuclear power plant.

The chainsaw section's
display looks like a butcher's stall
selling various types of crocodile:
Makita, Husqvarna, Poulan . . . Thick festoons

of chainblade glitter rawly.
I hand my gift to the salesman,
a bearded giant, letting my wife explain.
As she talks, a glint comes into his eye:

Afraid? Afraid of what? Getting hurt?
He won't if he's in a right relation. Listen—
He leans towards me with a twinkling grin,
Molson-muscle swelling his green plaid shirt—

British, right? I nod. That question here
puts my guard up, like *Are you Jewish?* did
in England where it meant *So you're a yid*,
at least to my hypersensitive ear,

as *British* here means—but I'm being paranoid;
he's got some other axe to grind: *King Arthur* . . .
Now there was a male mother,
nourishing his men on his own blood,

know what I'm saying? I don't. *Sir Bors, Gawain* ...
The warrior's gone dead in the modern male ...
I signal my wife *Let's go,* to no avail:
Your wild man's hurting ... *I can feel his pain* ...

Old stags like me can help young bucks like you—
and it dawns on me I'm hearing
something I might have heard in a drum-filled clearing
on Bill Moyers, ten years ago—

How about I show you how to use it;
stop by your place some morning? I'd be glad to.
You could cut my— I cut him off: *No thank you,*
and turn, leaving the chainsaw. *Wait one minute!*

I'll make you a deal:
take the saw home for free;
buck some blowdowns before you drop a tree.
Live with it, let it settle, get a feel;

keep it a year, then if you want it, pay—
you'll know where to find me—if not, fine.
I'm doing this for your sake, son, not mine—
I'm starting to feel trapped ... *I can't,* I bray,

I'm sick ... *I have this* ... *deepdown* ... *clumsiness* ...
cellular doggerel ... *my adolescence*
was one long chapter of accidents—
this finger pruned by a door, the rest all thumbs,

my left arm propeller-chopped like sushi;
see? The world was my banana skin.
I cracked my collarbone on a trampoline.
I caught dysentery from a bottle of Vichy.

In the birthing room, when the nurse
gave me the clippers, it took me
not one snip, not two, but three
to cut our child's umbilicus.

Besides, I don't approve of cutting trees;
bad for the planet, don't you know? He nods:
Problem is, if you don't clear your woods,
they'll sure as hell clear you. That's how it is

here in America. Maybe where you're from
you get to live as if that wasn't so;
as if your needs all balanced long ago
and everything fits snugly in its home,

but things aren't like that here. We still need teeth,
and not to bite our nails, as I see you do.
Either you clear your woods or they'll clear you—
You said that! Listen: I'm afraid of death,

or, to be more exact, of my apparent
death-wish, or more accurate still,
my possibly damaged, definitely faltering will
to stay alive: each lapse an "accident."

That's all there is to say, except goodbye.
But as I turn again, he grabs my wife
who half seems to expect it: *Tell him, Eve;*
you gave it to him, now you tell him why!

*

Instead of an apple, the tree
grew a ripe chainsaw:
a shiny blue Makita.
The woman plucked it and gave it to me.

Since then I have cut through a number of things:
a stand of maple and an acre of alder,
several chips on my shoulder,
the mother of all apron strings . . .

On every part of its body, the maker
had slapped red warnings: **Stop!**
Danger of Death! I took it up
to the edge of our once-clear

mountain meadow,
and where the woods had jumped the stone wall,
and a blossoming red maple
stood waving at its own shadow,

I set the throttle and choke,
yanked the starter cord:
once, twice, three times, hard as I could,
and my dubious gift awoke.

CHAINSAW I

As though you held in your hands
the severed head of Orpheus
crying his own *sparagmos*;
the mutilated bower
falling, still in flower—

or your own split kingdom's
hybrid of lion and unicorn:
at once dismembering tooth
and clarifying horn.

THE APOSTATE

The mirror was oval like her face.
Almond eyes, the blue-black curls
an equivocal admirer
once plied his fingers through
wistfully, before letting go.

Outside, hedgerows glittered;
rosehips, ripening cobnuts,
stitched in like silk as if the county
had slid from a palace wall and settled there.
Why do I long to be here when I am here?

The church battens onto its hill . . . Inside
eyes found her, lingered furtively
as on a curving surface that reflected
subtly distorted images of themselves,
and in their fascination felt a fear:

would she dissolve in them or they in her?
Too much brimmed in her presence;
the convert's accusing innocence,
betrayal's incandescence,
as if in her gesture the abandoned scrolls

had spilt themselves in one self-immolating
flash of outrage. Everything felt it—
lectern, pulpit; surely the anxious
altar would sprout and buckle into a star,
Cranmer's prayerbook open onto a *Sh'ma*!

Herself, she felt their looks as an unclothing;
a difficult, necessary dream
of intimate exposure to a crowd
flaying her strangeness from her till she stood
naked, at once their victim and one of them.

Kneeling, she closed her eyes and prayed—
What is this burden that grows
heavier the more of it I shed?
Here is the vicar. His pink face
pokes from its white fallopian flower

glossy as a hatchling angel.
He warbles like a dove. Exotic Anglican
incense of lilies, willow, wavering reeds
purls through the rafters, thinly.
He lays the host out like a picnic tea.

She takes her place . . . Impossible
not to feel for once the word made flesh,
watching her kneel and drink . . .
It splinters through her.
Out in the jangling air

she feels invisible, dispersed,
as if the gold-lipped chalice
had swallowed her into itself;
into the iron and flagstones, the pitted pillars,
into the earth outside—and this is grace,

briefly: an unestrangement from the sunken
farmtracks bleached like vertebrae, the sour
haze of hop pollen, scarlet hunt
blotting into a field, the whites
of cricketers on the green

where Christ the umpire
smiles on an eternity
of Judasless elevens,
comfy in his floppy crucifix
of lambswool sweaters, his jolly crown of caps.

HOPS

When the drunk at the bar of the Royal Oak
glared into my face,
gripping his pint like a hand grenade
from which he'd just taken the pin,
and told me what he told me,

the pang I felt
was like the split that goes on riving
all the way down the trunk
from one sound blow to the wedge,
as though it had been there forever, waiting.

That was the last time I felt at home
in a country pub, therefore England;
that, for me, being England—
that badger-set gloom
with its little church organ of bottles and pumps,

where a dim light from the sconce lamps
tools the unfakeable ease
on figures who belong there,
simply, set on their stools like chessmen,
as calmly set in their ways,

while over the burrowy stalings of pipe-smoke, yeast,
ancestral piss from the Gents
flares the bitter, freshening smell of hops,
feudal and vital; the inexhaustible gold dust
of the true Anglican host.

I worked on the neighboring farm one summer,
hop-picking with a crew of Gypsies.
The twelve-acre pole-and-wire trellises,
diagrammatic in spring,
had spurted their vines:

ten thousand living maypoles
in a haze of hop dust.
We hacked our way down the rows,
bundling tangled armfuls
into the stripping and sorting machines.

The clustering bracts
were sticky as flypaper:
little papery pouches of yellow snuff.
We stuffed them into burlap sacks,
then hauled them off to the ovens.

Two weeks into the season
the head-dazing, sour-gold smell
was in us like our own spoor;
we moved through the drifts of late summer
sweating it like the musk of hop gods.

We were the gods of that place if anyone was—
the stubble-gold shire streaming through us;
in sleep, crashed out under oak trees,
our sticky hands still sorting
the gold-filled, bunched, shrunken heads—

Albion juju;
I was full of it then:
Malory, Holinshed,
King John's sunk ducats
sifting from gold to sand

to hop pollen . . .
I'm exorcising it now
with a backwoods ghost-fragrance
of birch beer and applejack
on a barn porch under black locusts

where thumb-sized hummingbirds
zoom through the crimson bee-balm
and whenever I move my pen
a fountain of goldfinches
splashes out of the bushes.

A TIE-DYE T-SHIRT

Home from prep school
in my short-trousered herringbone suit,
I counted hippies on the streets of Notting Hill.
In their crushed-velvet bell-bottoms
they moved like shaggy-hooved centaurs.
I tagged along with a group
drifting down the Portobello.
One of them, tall and slim with long black hair,
wore a tie-dye T-shirt;
the first I had ever seen:
yellow mainly, with starbursts of rose and lime-green.
He was playing a silver flute. I felt myself
in the presence of superior beings,
as Major Wynkoop said of the Cheyennes.

Now thirty years later
my daughter makes me a tie-dye T-shirt
from one of the kits they sell
in the kitschy Tinker Street head shops.
I put it on and a strange
tremor of happiness goes through me.
I've half a mind to crack open
one of the spiked pods on this Jimson Weed,

toss its seed-spurt into the air,
swallow what the gods let me catch,
and hallucinate a week or two
in the psychedelic spring meadow,
where goldfinches and rose-breasted grosbeaks
flit between the creamy shadblow
and the lime-green,
catkin-veiled birches.

THE BACKHOE

For Pia

Van Kleef had plowed the road, we'd cut a track
from the woodpile to the door, dug out the car,
shoveled where the hemlocks shook their sleeves
in thudding dollops on the ice-swollen eaves.
The yard was like a building site or boneyard:
a rubble of knuckles and skulls; we stood there,
the city couple, patting ourselves on the back
when the first heavy flakes of the second blizzard

came drifting in. And now all over again
things swell and soften. The gray debris
brightens, loses its edge in a luminous
myopic blur. A velvet of spectral moss,
as in some lush, subzero planet's scheme
for rot, spreads over the woodpile. Every tree
ridges its branches with a thick white vein
and after its brief thaw blankness's regime

clamps down again. This time it looks conclusive;
more scrupulous than before, the flakes
falling so fast a thick white darkness

blots the windows and a steady hiss
chafes at the hush: white noise . . . What can we do
but sit and watch ourselves vanish like two mistakes
under the whiteout brush? And now Van Kleef
calls up to say the snowplow can't get through:

"You'll have to wait for the backhoe. Don't know when—"
and the line goes dead.
                              Two days later. The sky's
been blue since then, dead calm,
as if it knew exactly how much harm
was necessary for our object lesson
in our own helplessness, and bore no actual malice,
except that the power's out too, that the pipes have frozen,
that seven blankets are seven times colder than one,

that the world outside's like the sea of glass
in Revelation: deadlocked, the only motion
hemlock shadows inching over the snow
and the apocalyptic glow—
jacinth, beryl, chrysolite—
spilling out from the clouds as the afternoon
swerves into evening . . . Hadn't we reached this impasse
somewhere before? Silence, the numbing white

solidified future pressing in,
doors out heavy as boulders at a tomb:

terminal blockage, ourselves
cooling like statues as though our lives
had parted already and moved on elsewhere
without us . . . We'd waited for the end to come
but it hadn't; and I think of what happened then
now, as a rumbling wakes us and we stare

out through the window, not quite sure
what a backhoe is, and even when it passes
not much the wiser; the house-high
cablights piercing in too blindingly
to make out more than its force and dazzle,
snow splitting like the sea in front of Moses
in two tall glittering plumes, the blacktop's raw
glisten ribboning back out over the hill.

BLUESTONE

For Michael Hofmann

After the glassworks failed and the dairy farms,
battening onto the shrapnel tracts
clearcut for the furnace, failed in turn,
and the last resort gave up its empty rooms
to chipmunks and rattlesnakes, the facts
dampened all but the simplest dreams:
scraping a living; tending a bit of garden.

I didn't think I'd like it but I did,
inexplicably, this neither soothing
nor somehow uplifting landscape
of wooded bluestone crags crannied
by hollows and gullies, where nothing
human ever quite flourishes or quite
abandons—as it doubtless should—all hope.

Pecoy Notch, Bear Mountain, Sugarloaf;
each a begrudging mother's stony teat
yielding nothing not strictly needed
and not everything that is: not love,
at best a vaguely nutritive sweat
on which her stonier offspring vaguely thrive:
stones best of all; black locusts that look dead

most of the year, then when they are won't fall
but stiffen to thin flint pillars; ironwood;
unrottable tamarack; spiky, rock-solid pear trees;
anything barbed or thorned, any animal
or for that matter human, less flesh and blood
than tooth or talon, bristle, antler or quill . . .
Porcupines abound, wild turkeys

clatter in droves, briefly turning the bluestone
into themselves. I see it less as landscape
than as the image of a residuum:
clean-etched, irreducible unillusion;
hard to like, harder to give up;
the durable part of pleasure, living on
after its acid bath in boredom.

CHAINSAW II

Gesang ist Dasein —Rilke

and given the little caring left to care
for the possibly even less worth caring for;
given how at any given moment
you or anyway I would probably rather

be doing nothing than what we're doing,
this at least has the merit
not just of drowning out the drone
of Being's involuntary effort not to drown

in Nothingness, but also
of bringing things back to first principles:
the need to carve out a niche for ourselves;
our singular relation to what we love.

And if song is existence,
one could do worse for the roar
of life being lived to the hilt
than a blade plunged in solid wood.

BIRCH TREE WITH CHAINSAW

For Pia

Five months; five cords of hardwood;
ash mostly, hickory, oak;
graying in the weather,
by April starting to rot,
outsides sodden by May,
too crumbly even to splinter.

But then to uncover the first layer:
white birch, bright with the whiteness
that whitens your hands like chalk;
flesh-colored wood still firm
in its sheath of papery bands,
flaw-lined like slubbed silk.

Five months . . . Our pilgrim winter
in the squalls of parenthood,
the money-storms of ownership;
hodding the muddy ruins of the woodpile—
fungus-gilled, webby with slimes—
load by load to the stove,

till I come to the layer of white birch;
dust-white, the bark still tight,
sparkling in its pin-shoal,
the logs so sprung a knock
all but sets them ringing on their rails
like blocks on a glockenspiel.

I remember it; my first
plunge-cut, the bellying trunk
too plump for the usual felling kerf,
a bride among her bridesmaids
in its copse of lithe saplings.
I plunged the blade in, circling till she gave . . .

Now five cords later, to exhume
these limbs again, the winter-rotted
burial rags and pulp all gone;
just these in their bone-bright dazzle
as though to remind us we'd left
something unruined or still to ruin.

I feed them into the fire,
glad of its brightening glass
as they loosen their storm of flames,
and I'm seeing it again
veining the blue air with its ore
in tangled, silver-white seams.

Before I cut it I touched the trunk
as if its belly might kick like yours—
remember?—thaw-pools glinting in the woods,
shadblows foaming, and there,
indestructible, leaning into the light,
the birch in its veil of buds.

LEO RISING

He doesn't believe in me.
His neighbor saw me here on the ridge,
but he doesn't believe his neighbor.
I watch him from my bluestone ledge

hacking blueberry scrub with a whetted scythe,
clearing red maples with a chainsaw
in his tie-dye T-shirt.
I watch him as the King of Sicilia

watches the King of Bohemia
or Koba watches Lev Bronstein,
and I step from my bluestone ledge
to my ledge of blue sky,

and I watch him
venturing an existence,
presuming to continue to exist,
and I put on my brazen glance,

my long knives and my brownshirt,
my coat of napalm,
my tank-pack of Agent Orange,
and I watch him

clearing his wilderness, watering
the deserts of Bohemia,
perpetuating the affront of his existence
in the rainbowy flim of his T-shirt,

and his unbelief calls me forth
in midsummer, in the month of Av,
and I enter
fruit, flower and leaf,

and I disclose myself:
a catastrophe of golds;
a drought-napped, bracken-maned
torrent of dry blades.

Goodbye words;
my faltering muse's
unevenly burning flame
has sputtered out, and now like Diocletian
I'm taking early retirement.

Homesteading:
goats, organic lettuce,
that's the project; and when I
buck blowdowns or shovel dung from a pickup,
I'll remember how you once

were all I
needed or anyway
wanted of the crack and grain
of real things; how in your loam they'd swell, split
and banner out into themselves . . .

Now you can
just be their names again:
bluestone, shiplap, whatever.
And if I write, it'll be with a seed drill;
a quatrain of greens per bed, no sweat.

The dirt road
dead-ends on wilderness;
sometimes at night you can hear
unearthly gabblings: Bear Mountain's coyotes
closing in on a kill. Pure poetry.

WATER

SESSIONS:

NEW

POEMS

THE SKATERS

Their town's the quaint one:
the board won't let it sprawl
more than a half mile from the green's
little pool table of grass and shiny tulips
where Santa lands in winter and the teens
play hackysack all summer. There's no mall,

no motel either,
which is just what they want;
they voted for the good life there;
they can afford it: no fast-food chain, no sixplex,
they'll quietly brag; no trailer park, no air-
or groundwater-fouling autoshop or plant . . .

You'll find all that here
in the next town along.
You'll know you've reached us when you pass
a smooth vast meadow with a thousand white pipes
curved down like candycane, venting the gas
from their buried garbage. Then all the usual wrong

do-able by men
to a stubborn landscape,

to settle it and make it pay,
goes reeling by; the usual aching and craving
risen on blasted granite and raw clay.
They point their finger and they call it rape,

and maybe they're right,
though from some viewpoints, folks
might think them hypocritical,
like how they bring their kids to the new Kiwanis
ice rink—the kids all slim and tall
from too little junk food (one of our little jokes)—

every damn weekend.
Not that they're not welcome—
anyone can come here that wants:
here's failure without the allure, here's the mirage
gone from marriage; beer guts slung over pants,
butts like boulders in spandex, hard mouths home

on weekend parole;
here the abused and creased,
the maimed-in-spirit, the tainted
(what by, no one remembers or cares anymore)
totter out on their blades to get reacquainted
with sheer effortless rapture, or at least

the idea of it:
that frictionless surface
gets scratched and bleared up before long,
then turns to a thick, gray, gravelly slurry . . .
which, we have to admit, is easier-going,
maybe because it reminds us of us,

though for a moment,
the page of ice still bare,
we're just like them again: all flow,
our stumblings still not written, the world so primed
we're back believing where we want to go
we'll get to, just by *wishing* ourselves there.

THE BLIGHT

What's there to say? We didn't care for him much,
and you can't exactly commiserate
with someone you don't just not love
but almost (admit it) hate.
So the news just hung over us
like the dud summer weather we'd had—
rain since June, the lawn sodden,
garden a bog, all slugs, late blight so bad
our sickened Beefsteak vines, our Sweet One Hundreds,
San Marzanos, the lot,
yellowed half black before the fruit had set,
which, when it did, began to bloat and rot
before it ripened—but like I say
(and not to speak ill of the dead)
we just didn't care for him,
which is probably all there is to be said.

THE QUESTION

We're eating outside with our friends,
Woodstock Buddhists; our kids and theirs
are lighting sticks on citronella candles
to throw them at the woods like burning spears;
the Rainbow Family of Living Light
are drumming in Magic Meadow; I've drunk enough
that all I want to do is close my eyes,
when a voice rings like a summons from the darkness:
my six-year-old son asking: "Dad,
is America good or bad?"

He's heard us talking; the litany:
stolen elections, torture memos, wars;
seen the picture of the hooded man—
Haj Ali, our oppressor-victim,
arms spread, posed on his box
like Jesus on his mountain
blessing the peacemakers
(but for the dangling wires)
and wants to know whose side he's on:
his own or someone else's side against him . . .

What can I say? *That depends*
on what you mean by "good" or "bad"
or for that matter "America,"
which might be a fool and his goons
war-gaming in the White House,
but might be, say, the Women in Black
down on the Green with their banner, "Bring Our Troops Back,"
or the Rainbow People up in the meadow
drumming in the full moons,
or might just be us and our friends . . . ?

He's waiting for his answer.
I open my mouth to speak
but something stalls me; a strange
heaviness on my tongue
as if after all I'd pledged silence
or struck some nocturnal pact
over whatever act,
doubtful or downright wrong,
secures our presence here,
and I can't seem to say a damn thing,

and he drifts away, back to his game
of fending off the trees
that look as though they'd marched up the hill
to mass at the edge of our lawn
while we sat here talking,

and a dim shame
clouds in as if there were really something to do
other than drink and chill
and listen to the drums beat
and try to keep our eyes open.

STORM

Driving towards them at dusk
I thought they were tree stumps:
first-growth hemlocks, storm-felled
decades ago, their trunks carted off for lumber,

but I had my dimensions wrong:
what the twilight had rounded out
and turned to rotting wood was flat
mossed-over stone. They were gravestones,

tilted that way by frost. I drove on,
out of the wind and lightning
my mind had conjured in error.
It was a warm evening; lilac on the air.

Motels along the Turnpike
had lit up neon signs;
Welcome, they pulsed in scarlet.
Welcome. Welcome. Welcome.

DIDO IN HELL

I was in woods;
twilight, the green glow
of swamp-maple leaves, dank air,
then that figure,
unmistakable, moving out of shadow

towards me:
my almost wife;
a gaping wound at her breast, her face
white, staring, expressionless,
in her hand the hunting knife

I'd given her; blood-blackened now. A sound—
half sob, half hiss—
broke from my throat: it was true then.
What I'd heard was true: the measure taken.
Listen, I'm not responsible for this

I heard myself utter,
I never lied to you—my voice
rising, unsteady—*did I? did I?*
She stood in silence.
I had no choice! You knew I had no choice!

You knew . . . She'd gone though,
faded back into the woods.
Night fell. There were no stars;
only this tangling blackness
and my echoing words.

BLUES FOR SAMSON

My stylist
calls me darling,
says Hi I'm Dee, and asks what I'd like today, smiling.
My hair back, I tell her, my precious locks,
thick and unruly and glossy as they were
before I was fleeced.

Her laughter
as she switches
the clippers on, brings back that sweet-throated witch's
who comforted me as only your enemy can
in the days of my strength, when I smote
hip and thigh in a great slaughter.

Her nice eyes
by and by rest
on mine in the mirror. She leans in, letting her breast
brush against me. She knows her middle-aged man;
playing me like some trailer Delilah,
and I feel it rise;

the old blunt
want-instrument
that always and only wanted what it shouldn't;

Gaza, Timna, my Valley girl
who spilled me in broad daylight. I must have reckoned
the sun shone out of her cunt.

Too long now
bereft of it,
a woman's hands in my hair, or what's left of it,
is all I seem to require of love,
and all I'll spill is a tip, Dee; big as my straitened
circumstances allow,

for Dee, once
my head wasn't bare
as that cornfield after the foxes I set on fire
rampaged through it, or the orchards and olive groves
I flattened with my slat-armored D9 'dozer,
but maned like a lion's.

GOLEM

I'm looking for the crack
where the yellow jackets nest.
I stumbled on it last summer
out here in the snakeroot
between the fence and the forest.
I had no idea
what it was that came boiling
out of that hidden fissure
in a sudden, upturned
blizzard of scalding gold,
only that its stings
were not the whiplash
of reflex, but some fury
my deadweight must have roused
and in one long crackling flash
of white-hot letters
branded across my brow,
intent on rousing me: I ran,
flailing, incandescent,
in my own wheeling halo,
my suit of lightning, fire
racing through my astounded

body, my dumbstruck tongue
unscabbarding its word
up out of living bedrock
all that bright morning.

—We had a fight. She threw her water at me.
My skin still feels hot
where it hit me: a splash-brand tingling

across my forehead—*What was the fight about?*
I don't remember. Nothing important.
The water's what I remember. It made me feel . . .

—*Yes?*—I want to say impotent
but that's not quite it; a stranger
debilitation as though I'd

absorbed some bone-melting toxin from her anger:
I can see the flung water still,
its chrome fingers probing towards me, elongating

like silvery staghorn coral,
and the splash, the impact, I can still feel that,
the soft catastrophic crash

like being spat at:
cracher . . . I like the French word better;
juices your mouth and gives you the double disaster,

the spat-at but also the spitter,
like in *Nostromo*; that moment when Señor Hirsch,
hung from a beam by his elbows,

spits in his torturer's face, splash-crash,
—*You see yourself as her torturer?*
—No, but there does seem

some time-bending sorcery in the gesture;
a retrofit, let's say, of the crime to the punishment,
backwardly flooding what one had thought quite harmless

with downright evil intent.
I mean, I had no more idea
of what I had coming than the boy in the myth

Ceres spattered with wet grain for mocking her,
turning him into a scuttling lizard, as if
he could have known or imagined what it might mean

to step out, to walk his little life
into the ten-lane highway of a goddess's existence;
or Ascalaphus, splashed by Proserpine,

etched to a screech owl in the instant's
acid-burn of underworld waters,
or Actaeon

who did nothing worse
than lose his way out hunting in a wood
and stumble on Diana skinny-dipping

when *splash!*—the water antlered into his forehead
as she flung a scooped handful in rage,
as if being divine merely meant

being a flood in abeyance, an englobed deluge
primed for the instant engulfment
of anything too radically not itself,

at which the branching—*Excuse me, I think at this point
you ought to tell me what the fight was about—*
—at which the branching horns splashed out from his brow,

his ears furred over and sharpened, his hands and feet
hardened to hooves, and off he stagger-galloped
chased by his own dogs

who sank their fangs in his hide and ripped
—*What was the fight about?*
—I told you, I don't remember, besides,

who ever really knows what a fight was about?
I mean you go in thinking it's one thing, then later
discover it was all along

some totally unrelated matter . . .

WOODPILE

The tolerant structure of a woodpile.
Two or more rows deep, each row end-stopped
by crisscrossing pairs of parallel logs
stacked up in columns: its one formal touch, and that optional,
otherwise a matter of simple accretion;
long or high as you want it; the piled chunks,
whether trapezoid in section, or half-moon, or witch-silhouette;
knobbed or bulbous, split like crocodile jaws,
or rock-hard uncrackable knots; whether
red oak, black cherry or yellow birch,
bearing each other's polyglot oddities
with an agglomerated strength, the opposite
of the engineer's soaring, cross-braced,
precision-cut glass and steel.

I make mine under a maple in the backyard,
from the five cords dumped there each year
by the cord-wood seller's dump truck. Mindless work—
stooping, grabbing, chucking, stacking—
but I like it: the guaranteed satisfaction,
the exact ratio of effort to result;
how you can't fail at this if you put in the effort
any more than you can fake it if you don't,

and its endlessly forgiving form, that too; how a misplaced
or mischosen log doesn't matter,
how even when you think you're done
there's always room for another one on top;
everything coming out right in the end, more or less,
however clumsy its creator.

MR. W.H.

Not that bloodlines,
family or otherwise
have ever meant much to me,
but at fifty one wants forebears
almost as much as heirs,
and even though the oblivion
we're headed for is doubtless
total, it feels somewhat
lonely heading there orphaned,
or lonelier than not.

Of course every poet
appoints his own ancestors
but that's one thing if you're Auden
enlisting Byron, another
if you're nobody claiming Auden.
Let me present, then
(like one of those not quite kosher
relations in Jane Austen),
my mite of collateral evidence
connecting me with Wystan.

First, prep school; first cell in that hive
"whose honey is fear and worry"—

and not just any old holding pen
for the immature British toff,
but St. Edmund's School, Hindhead, Surrey;
the school he and I both attended.
I doubt much had changed
in the fifty years between us,
from the stony puntabout
we waited on every third Sunday

worried our distant parents
might forget or not bother to come,
to the horsehair mattresses
we lay on, groping our way
to that potent formula
of pleasure, shame and repression
Freud had construed long before
as the jet-fuel of civilization—
the energy-flight from Eros
to monuments, railways, war;

and that listless indoor
golf course of a landscape's
gravel drives and laurel hedges,
its buffed-to-a-gloss silver birches,
its insinuating mildness
that at best tamed us
into our bourgeois thrall to the "ever so comfy,"

not to mention our *penchant* for comfortable rhymes;
at worst so mimetically maimed us
as to make our—or anyway my—

utter loathing for it
a form of self-loathing . . .
Fast-forward twenty-five years
to my second exhibit:
a campus in New England—
old England on steroids;
the hills pumped up into mountains,
the little creosote potting sheds
swollen to ark-sized dairy barns anchored on meadows
big as counties.

I taught there in the nineties;
Auden in the forties.
Freshmen danced for him naked.
By my time the place
was a front line in the battle
between the cerebral interest
and that of the, shall we say,
mailed fist?
Freedom—of thought, speech, dissent—
versus the President.

Freedom was losing badly:
tenure abolished, rumors

of impropriety spread,
eighteen professors fired;
the letter describing their protest
as *vengeful and selfish*;
you had to sign it
or risk being fired yourself.
Well, it wasn't Berlin or Spain
and doubtless wouldn't have merited

one line from Wystan's pen,
though the "set mask of rectitude"
seems apropos—though again
the "important Jew" who stripped it
has been all but stripped himself
from the approved shelf
by the professionally offended,
for putting (he might have put it)
the eros in generosity,
and though it isn't Vienna either

("Anna *bei Gestapo*")
there's a certain chill in the air;
Mastema, god of hatred, back in business,
working with equal zest
in the oppressor's uniform
and the rags of the oppressed;
you can track him by the bodies

dumped like a monster's feces
in unexpected places;
while the last big thing that isn't yet ourselves,

out in the cold too long,
its face up against the glass,
window-crashes the party; and don't get me wrong:
I've seen those self-pitying monster-eyes
staring back out of mirrors;
I've felt the mounting
voluptuous hatred, the swell
of violence surge and foam from the littlest wound
to liquidate, if it could, conjectured
enemy-comrades, classes, whole nationalities,

and I accept my latent
guilt in the future
necessary murder
of my dearest neighbors; my hand,
if not yet dripping blood, at any rate ink-stained,
having said which, it's still Dame Kind—
unkillable *Tellus Mater*—
I choose to think of
as I look out over the barn porch
where the old hollow-hearted

crippled apple, all dad—what's the word?
daddock—all daddock and moss
and sagging, swirling-grained bulges,
stands like a fossilized
beggarwoman or sage:
dead, I'd thought, till I noticed
a cluster of green apples
like a branchful of underworld eyes
coolly regarding
my empty page.

THE EVENT

But did you imagine it would wait,
its fuse already lit, while you labored
day and night for the exact word
to name what it was? Did you imagine it wouldn't
become without you what it hadn't with,
soonness always the point (you knew that though,
didn't you, didn't you? which is doubly tough).
Let go, ringed in its absence; crater or wreath:
all but posthumous now, your craving's token;
compliments to a former belle
not much noticed, whose heart lives in its aches
as in a peach-stone the fire of peaches . . .
Things'll be fine, as far as you can tell,
but that show's over now, that wave has broken.

IT ISN'T ME

It isn't me, he'd say,
stepping out of a landscape
that offered, he'd thought, the backdrop
to a plausible existence
until he entered it; *It's just not me*,
he'd murmur, walking away.

It's not quite me, he'd explain,
apologetic but firm,
leaving some job they'd found him.
They found him others: he'd go,
smiling his smile, putting
his best foot forward, till again

he'd find himself reluctantly concluding
that this, too, wasn't him.
He wanted to get married, make a home,
unfold a life among his neighbors' lives,
branching and blossoming like a tree,
but when it came to it, *It isn't me*

was all he seemed to learn
from all his diligent forays outward.

And why it should be so hard
for someone not so different from themselves,
to find what they'd found, barely even seeking;
what gift he'd not been given, what forlorn

charm of his they'd had the luck to lack,
puzzled them—though not unduly:
they lived inside their lives so fully
they couldn't, in the end, believe in him,
except as some half-legendary figure
destined, or doomed, to carry on his back

the weight of their own all-but-weightless stray
doubts and discomforts. Only sometimes,
alone in offices or living rooms,
they'd hear that phrase again: *It isn't me,*
and wonder, briefly, what they were, and where,
and feel the strangeness of being there.

WATCHER

In the lit space
between a fluorescent Chanel ad
and a cavern of duty-free Steuben,
herself less flesh and blood
than scent, it seems, and cut glass,
she settles in with her iPod
and a magazine.

He glances over;
feels it, that almost
outraged yearning, as if
for something he once possessed
and might yet recover
if he can just
make her turn for one brief

reciprocal look,
and he looks again, then again, each glance
a spray of sand
against an immense, glazed indifference
till at last, slowly, as if being tugged awake
out of its own separate trance,
her body stirs, and her hand

touches her things—
phone, laptop, coat—
and draws them in close
like some watchful spirit
armored in bracelets and rings,
and that's all. It's not till she hears her flight
called in that air-brushing voice

fashioned, he half imagines,
for summoning bored gods
and goddesses back to Olympus
on their own private clouds,
that she stands and deigns
to let the bright blue diodes
of her eyes rest on his

for a moment's glance,
then turns, the gesture
slow and deliberate,
as if to show him everything he'd ever
wanted but couldn't have; swans, stallions, dolphins
glittering as she takes it with her
calmly down the walkway to her gate.

A PEELED WAND

September clearness, insects
glinting on the far shore;
bullfrogs, red-winged blackbirds—
the dial tone of summer—
bubbling up through the evening air . . .
Out on the water a snapper
snags a V of ripples
towards us—no, not a snapper . . .
We slow to a halt
as whatever it is circles closer
till we see him, suddenly clear in the water,
the curves of his half-submerged brow
bulging on the surface
like the smooth bulges on tree trunks
loggers call cat-face flaws;
forelegs working beneath him,
leisurely, as though walking on air;
and now, closer still,
in the bluestone-bottomed shallows,
he rises, holding aloft
the dripping boat of his head,
calmly scanning the bankside thickets,
then steps from the water,

lumbering right across our path,
and with two audible snips,
snips through an alder sapling
(the young bark still glossy brown)
in a salad of its own leaves
and shoulders it back to the shallows,
where, with the same unconcern,
he strips off and chews, one by one,
every twig and leaf,
washing each mouthful down
with a sip of our silver water
then glides off
for a between-courses swim
halfway across the reservoir,
paddle-tail wafting him
through a reflected mountain . . .
Winter now;
snow like wool, as the psalm says, mists like ashes.
I think of him out there again
in the late summer evening sweetness
of sumac and goldenrod,
swimming unhurriedly back
for the tender bark of the sapling;
turning the stick with his hands, nibbling
the tight skin clear from the greenwood—
all but a few tough inches at the thick end
left like a leather-bound hilt—

then with a last look around him
at the lilac-edged ring of mountains
and the sky like a jeweler's tray
with a sun and an opal moon
and two or three choice stars,
heading off back where he came from,
fanning a fishtail wake on the water
and leaving behind him the peeled wand
which I have here in my hand.

—But go back a moment
to that other dream,
about the river, remember,

the one half-hidden by trees, that time
you thought you'd dried up
—Yes, all cresses and willows

green-lit black water, swift and deep
—Narrow, you said
—Well, not the Hudson, an English river

*—And you above it—*Astride
more like, as if it flowed
from my own, you know, my loins

*—Which felt?—*Oh god, good!
—Like in that stranger's garden
in last night's dream?

—Go on . . .
— Your irrigation lines dry,
your own garden dead

—Which was most irrigating. Sorry.
—*You followed the lines to the stream*
which also turned out to be dry,

then climbed back upstream—Updream
—*Way back, yes? To a fork*
where all the water ran down the other fork

to the stranger's garden, which you say was like
—Paradise! The clear water brimming in fonts,
spilling over the beds, which stilled it

in ingots of gold squash, pepper plants;
held it in delicate scalloped or spear-tipped leaves,
muskmelons heavy and scented like babies' heads,

tomatoes big as . . . big as boxing gloves;
I mean you could feel the surge of unimpeded
existence in every blissed-out sunburst corolla,

every collard leaf loaded
with waterglobes gleaming like gems on a shelf . . .
My god!—*Any idea who this stranger was?*

—None.—*You're sure?*—You want me to say myself
don't you?—*Do I?*—Some ghost-self perhaps,
one who'd either been spared whatever crime,

whatever irreparable lapse
from grace or luck that fork upstream represents
or else was himself the water thief,

as though I'd somehow stolen my own existence
from under my nose; somehow siphoned it off
elsewhere, like the Jordan waters

bled out into the roses of the Negev;
is that what you're saying? The dream
an effort, then, to reconcile certain polarities;

desert blossom, for instance, with suicide bomb,
or General Electric's "We Bring Good Things to Light,"
with the death-sludge they dumped in the Hudson,

or for that matter the British Mandate—
—*You're losing me*—Well, but it's true,
as heir to whatever misdeeds my own

triple axis—Anglo-American-Jew—
occasioned or outright did
before I became, as it were,

CEO of Myself Incorporated,
I might indeed wish to reconcile, even equate
certain opposites; villain and victim

tourist and terrorist; spitter even, and spat-at . . .
—*Which brings us back, does it not,*
to your fight. I think you should really—

—Like I said, who ever knows what a fight was about?
You go in thinking it's oil or land, and then later
discover it was all along only ever

about water . . .

THE RUINED HOUSE

We passed these places
when we came this way before:
stone-towered fortress-farmhouses
going slowly to pieces
in a desolation of broom,
ilex and wild roses;
windows boarded, the spill
of terraces brambled over,
crumbling back into hill.

Someone explained it:
reform of the *mezzadrile*;
the old feudal peasantry
unbound from their vineyards,
their olive groves and beehives;
upgraded to wage-slaves.
No reason not to be elsewhere,
they left the land in droves,
went where the living was easier . . .

I had given up
a servitude of my own
to a no less exacting *padrone*;

Oh, I had broken
strong indentures, forsaken
the path of glory,
the discipline of the line,
for these paths of least resistance;
the sentence for the *sentiero*.

Now ten years later
I come full circle to find
the place in strange remission;
a posthumous *dolce vita*:
the houses newly young;
glazed, painted, repointed;
cisterns cleaned, doors rehung
a libidinous gleam
of Volvos under arbors.

So why do my spirits sink
and why do they rise again
at the one house all in ruins?
Why this gladness,
this unexpected relief
at the vine-spewing casements
and the front room's rank smash of rubble,
and the great, dank, black-fruited fig tree
erupting out of the roof?

DUST

We were children here,
biblical siblings,
mauling each other on the cave-floor
of the workshop and the playroom.

Adults now,
together on housework detail:
we roll up the old white living-room rug,
lug it out on our shoulders

like the hide of some ancient beast
we'd tracked down in its lair,
slinging it up between the fence and the toolshed,
and laying into it, each with a thick iron bar,

you on one side, me on the other,
slamming it hard, with a thud
and a burst of dust at each blow, the dust
chalking the air till our eyes

smart, and we're choking and have to stop for it to clear,
then stand there watching it
floating like some glinting amorphous ghost,
down the garden and over the fields below.

BITTERSWEET

In your book, success
was a dirty word, wealth
even dirtier, fame
not to be uttered;
the work was all that mattered.
I took that to heart, I guess,
in my own monkish fashion:
"So much to say no to
before you can start to say yes"
having long been my motto.
No, for instance,
to the bittersweet
I'm trying to extirpate
from under the garden fence.
I'd thought nothing of it
except that its berries
might brighten the wires in fall
like a coat of arms on a wall,
but it's taken over the place:
lost, one has to assume,
in the delirium
of its own joyous work
of making the universe
or at any rate this fence

a monument, shall we say,
to its own magnificence;
and not just this mass of scarlet, orange-winged berries
seething like a swarm of underworld bees,
or the intractable tanglings
of vines like stiffened springs,
but these astounding roots also:
blood-bright, trailing their corpse-hair capillaries
down through the topsoil. I yank them out
only to find they've coiled right down through the shale
into solid bedrock,
leaving a lizard tail in each crack
potent enough to grow the whole lizard back
just in case there remained any doubt, any question
as to the error, the sheer utter folly of planning
a garden of one's own
where bittersweet has grown.

INDUSTRY BAY

Here's your grandson clowning in the ocean;
scuttling out of the waves then bossing them back.
He looks more like you every minute;
beetling his brow in the same mock frown you made.
Here's a hammock without you lying in it;
a sea-grape tree without you in its shade.
And here's me, taking the measure of your absence;
failing again; stalled like that restless palm top
flapping its chicken feathers in the sun
while overhead some wide-winged ocean bird
rises on the breezes without effort
as if to tell me: *this is how it's done* . . .

THING ONE AND THING TWO

The gelding knife
they showed me on the farm
was an adjustable, steel-tendoned instrument,
part plier, part caliper,
with two raw-edged sickle moons
that opened on springs and closed
like crab claws: the deed, it appeared,
requiring as complex a harm
as the harm it opposed.

The box of hard-core porn
I found in the woods
was softened by rain,
its pinks and purples leached to bluey grays,
bloated flesh splitting open
under my fumbling, impatient touch,
with a reeking sweetness.
I was queasy with it for days.
Then I went there again.

The billy goat
was up on his hind legs, in rut;
blethering, poking his tongue out, frotting the fence,

slit-pupiled yellow eyes rolling, coat
glistening gold like an archbishop's cloak
from his damascene drip and drool.
The farmer cocked his adamantine tool.
"Snip snip and Bob's your auntie,"
as my father used to joke.

My son
sprawls in my lap, naked,
frolicking with his own
delinquent cat in a hat
while things one and two run amok
in his bedtime book,
and all this comes back
as an urge—I suppress it—
to stop him.

DOG DAYS

Blizzard died. I'm remembering
his limitless affection;
how he constantly gave you the chance to open your heart,
to thaw some of the ice around it;
how I failed to respond; knowing I should, but unable,
as if some crucial defeat would thereby be registered,
though even as I complained about him tramping mud all over
    the house,
or filling the snow in the yard with piss stains and frozen turds
or getting his muzzle full of porcupine quills,
or jumping bang through the screen door, or licking the butter,
or costing a fortune in pills and shots;
how, behind my posture of annoyance, behind my frosty hostility,
I knew him to be a princely spirit, magnanimous;
knew it from how he greeted me after every rebuff
with his jumps and nuzzles;
every day saying "This is your chance to show love . . ."
Why couldn't I show it?
Why this sense that good as it might have been,
it would also have been a violation of the natural order
or my own personal order?
I see him,
trotting ahead in the woods,

the big white plume of his tail bobbing up and up
like an irrepressible fountain, then vanishing
as he thundered off after a squirrel.
When he slept, his flank would start quivering;
he'd draw back his ears and his muzzle, and moan with delight,
chasing the squirrel again in his dreams.
Once, while I lay on the couch, flattened by depression,
he came and placed his paw in my hand,
and made a pitiful, pitying baying sound.
I did feed and water him, even cleaned up his shit once in a while,
but always with a dutiful air, an aggrieved look of martyrdom,
as though afraid our household would collapse
if someone in it didn't preserve a certain stiffness,
a certain chilliness in regard to the purely creaturely.

WATER SESSIONS III

You made up?—We just let it go.
It seemed suddenly possible:
a change of mood like a change of season;

nothing in our control
other than being ours to accept or not
—*And you did?*—We went for a walk

up to the lookout.
Below us already vivid
powdery bud-sprays rolled like smoke through the valley.

I hadn't realized spring had arrived.
Under the ridge-snow a sheet
of meltwater slid over grasses and mosses,

new ferns scoping up through the rubble of slate . . .
That other kingdom, going about its business,
there for you if you want it, waiting

like a long-suffering friend, or former mistress;
post-diluvian, sexless, second best,
knowing your weaknesses, forgiving them . . .

—*And so?*—It started raining. We kissed
in the damp shelter of a cliff,
dodging crashing icicles. Luminous

ice-glazed birches dripped and wept. Far off,
curving over the river,
the bridge lay glittering like a ring.

And that none of this, not the rain,
nor this unexpected reprieve,
would go on forever seemed strangely . . .

—*Yes?*—Fair, I guess. Fair enough.

TO A PESSIMIST

It's true: the chances
that good luck won't stop dropping in your lap
are, as they are of most things, mostly against;
that whether looked at from this or the far side of fences,
the grass is basically ashes,
and that half-full or -empty, the best-laid glass
invariably smashes.

But before you bury
your head in a dune of Zoloft,
remember—speaking of odds—the sheer oddness
of being brought into this sunlit, sublunary
existence's bosom
out of the black, like some ancient ironwood's
improbable blossom.

To be born, to have hollowed
this singular passage, the exact
outline of yourself, through the rock of ages,
argues, does it not, that one might be allowed
if not to aspire
to outright happiness, then at least to resist
abject despair?

Your house will fall down, for sure,
followed—who knows?—by the sky itself,
but not today, and probably not tomorrow,
and bear in mind also that despite the law
that returns must diminish,
the gods, when they act at all, have been known to bless
as well as to punish.

STONES

I'm trying to solve the problem of the paths
between the beds. A six-inch cover
of cedar chips that took a month to lay
rotted in two years and turned to weeds.
I scraped them up and carted them away,
then planted half a sack of clover seeds
for a "living mulch." I liked that: flowers
strewn along like stars, the cupid's bow
drawn on each leaf like thumbnail quarter moons,
its easy, springy give—until it spread
under the split trunks framing off each bed,
scribbling them over in its own
green graffiti . . . I ripped it out
and now I'm trying to set these paths in stone.
It isn't hard to find: the ground here's littered
with rough-cut slabs, some of them so vast
you'd think a race of giants must have lived here
building some bluestone Carnac or Stonehenge,
us their dwindled offspring, foraging
among their ruins . . . I scavenge
lesser pieces; pry them from the clutches
of tree roots, lift them out of ditches,
filch them from our own stone wall

guiltily, though they're mine to take,
then wrestle them on board the two-wheeled dolly
and drag them up the driveway to the fence,
where, in a precarious waltz, I tip
and twist them backward, tilting all their weight
first on one corner, then the other
and dance them slowly through the garden gate.
The hard part's next, piecing them together;
a matter of blind luck and infinite pains:
one eye open for the god-given fit—
this stone's jagged key to that one's lock—
the other quietly gauging how to fudge it:
split the difference on angles, cram the gaps
with stone-dust filler; hoping what the rains
don't wash away, the frost will pack and harden . . .
A chipmunk blinks and watches from his rock,
wondering if I've lost my mind perhaps.
Perhaps I have; out here every day,
cultivating—no, not even that;
tending the inverse spaces of my garden
(it's like a blueprint now, for Bluebeard's castle),
while outside, by degrees, the planet slips
—a locking piece—into apocalypse,
but somehow I can't tear myself away:
I like the drudgery; I seem to revel
in pitting myself against the sheer
recalcitrance of the stones; using

their awkwardness—each cupped or bulging face,
every cockeyed bevel and crooked curve,
each quirk of outline (this one a cracked lyre,
that one more like a severed head)—
to send a flickering pulse along the border
so that it seems to ripple round each bed
with an unstonelike, liquid grace:
"the best stones in the best possible order"
or some such half-remembered rule in mind,
as if it mattered, making some old stones
say or be anything but stone, stone, stone;
as if these paths might serve some purpose
aside from making nothing happen; as if
their lapidary line might lead me somewhere—
inward, onward, upward, anywhere
other than merely back where I began,
wondering where I've been, and what I've done.

BLUEBERRIES

I'm talking to you old man.
Listen to me as you step inside this garden
to fill a breakfast bowl with blueberries
ripened on the bushes I'm planting now,
twenty years back from where you're standing.
It's strictly a long-term project—first year
pull off the blossoms before they open,
second year let them flower, watch the bees
bobbing in every bonnet,
but don't touch the fruit till year three,
and then only sample a handful or two . . .
Old man I'm doing this for you!
You know what they say about blueberries:
blood-cleansing, mood-lifting memory-boosters;
every bush a little fountain of youth
sparkling with flavonoids, anthocyanin . . .
I've spent all summer clearing brush,
sawing locust poles for the frames,
digging in mounds of pine needles, bales of peat moss—
I thought I'd do it while I still could.
You can do something for me in turn:
think about the things an old man should;
things I've shied away from, last things.

Care about them only *don't* care too
(you'll know better than I do what I mean
or what I couldn't say, but meant).
Reconcile, forgive, repent,
but don't go soft on me; keep the faith,
our infidels' implicit vow:
"Not the hereafter but the here and now . . ."
Weigh your heart against the feather of truth
as the Egyptians did, and purge its sin,
but for your own sake, not your soul's.
And since the only certain
eternity's the one that stretches backward,
look for it here inside this garden:
Blueray, Bluecrop, Bluetta, Hardy Blue;
little fat droplets of transubstantiate sky,
each in its yeast-misted wineskin, chilled in dew.
This was your labor, these are the fruits thereof.
Fill up your bowl old man and bring them in.

INDEX
OF
TITLES
AND
FIRST
LINES

Note: Titles are in SMALL CAPS.

Printed in the USA
CPSIA information can be obtained
at www.ICGtesting.com
LVHW091145150724
785511LV00005B/549

9 780374 535506